SEA
ANIMALS

written by Priscilla Hannaford
illustrated by Studio Boni/Galante

Ladybird

Contents

Introduction

Many different kinds of animals live in the sea. Some of them are tiny. Others are huge. Whales are the biggest animals on Earth.

You are unlikely to see a whale unless you are on a boat. But you can see other sea animals by going to the coast, where many make their homes beside the sea.

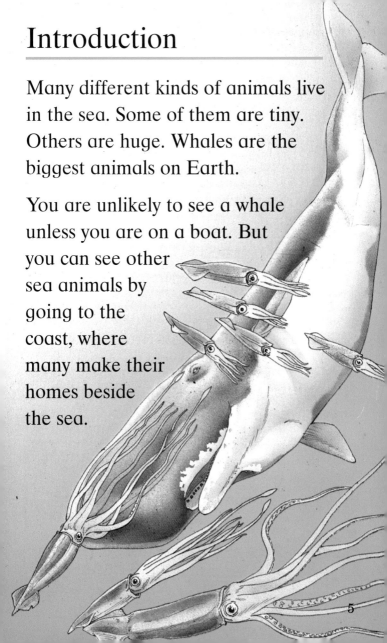

The Sea

The sea often seems to move on its own. Waves make the water go up and down. They are caused by the wind blowing over the sea.

Tides also make the sea move. When it is high tide the sea comes right up to the top of the beach. As the tide goes down, it leaves a line of seaweed behind.

Many birds make nests by the sea, including some gulls. Gulls are common throughout the world, with over forty different kinds.

Pearl

When sand gets inside a **mollusc** shell, the mollusc can cover it with a shell-like material to form a pearl.

Gulls eat fish and small animals, like crabs. They eat rubbish that people have thrown out, as well. This is why they like to follow boats across the ocean.

Going to sea

You can often see sea animals more easily from a boat. But you must be careful – the sea can be a dangerous place.

Seashore Life

Along the coastline there are beaches, coves, bays and cliffs. Some beaches are sandy. Sand is made from rocks and seashells that have been broken into tiny pieces by the sea over a long time.

Curlews jab their long beaks into the sand to pull out worms and molluscs.

Curlews

8

Along the shore you may see rock pools. Animals that live in these have to **adapt** to the rise and fall of the tide every day. Sea anemones and other animals cling tightly to rocks so that they are not swept away as the tide goes out.

Shrimps have ten legs, but they aren't very good at crawling. They are much better at swimming.

Shrimp

Crabs raise their eyes to look around, and lower them when they are not in use.

Crab

Fish

Fish live in all the seas of the world. They are very adaptable creatures and come in many different shapes and sizes. Some, like flying fish, swim near the surface of the water. Others, like the tripod fish, prefer to live in the cold, dark water near the sea floor.

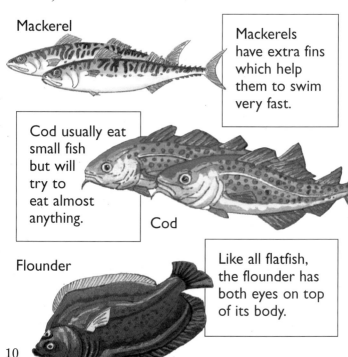

Mackerel

Mackerels have extra fins which help them to swim very fast.

Cod usually eat small fish but will try to eat almost anything.

Cod

Flounder

Like all flatfish, the flounder has both eyes on top of its body.

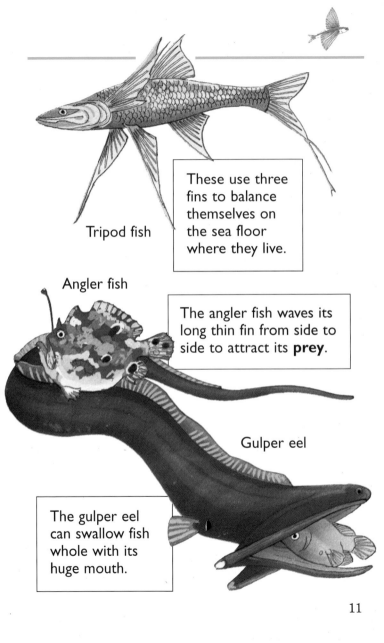

Tripod fish

These use three
fins to balance
themselves on
the sea floor
where they live.

Angler fish

The angler fish waves its
long thin fin from side to
side to attract its **prey**.

Gulper eel

The gulper eel
can swallow fish
whole with its
huge mouth.

11

Sharks

Sharks swim in every one of the
Earth's oceans, and even one or two
of the bigger rivers. Some sharks are
gentle and harmless. Others, like the
great white shark, are fierce hunters.
Sharks were the first fish to **evolve**.

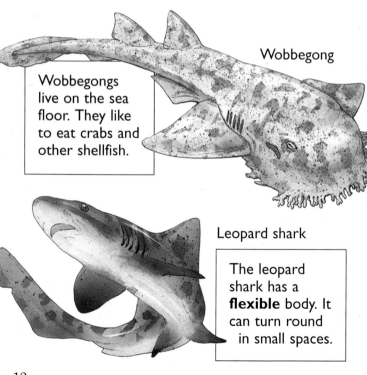

Wobbegong

Wobbegongs
live on the sea
floor. They like
to eat crabs and
other shellfish.

Leopard shark

The leopard
shark has a
flexible body. It
can turn round
in small spaces.

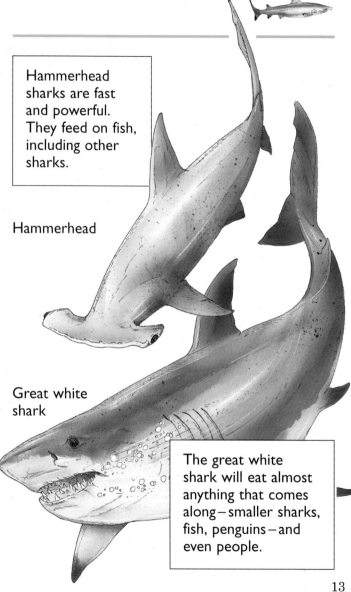

Hammerhead sharks are fast and powerful. They feed on fish, including other sharks.

Hammerhead

Great white shark

The great white shark will eat almost anything that comes along – smaller sharks, fish, penguins – and even people.

13

Sea Mammals

Walruses, seals, sea lions and sea
otters all live in, or by, the sea. These
animals are not fish, they are
mammals like us. They breathe air
and give birth to live young.

Walrus

Walruses live in groups of
about one hundred animals.
They eat mainly shellfish.

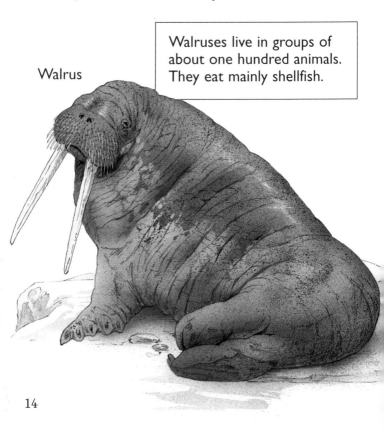

Seals can hold their breath
for a long time as they dive
underwater in search of fish
to eat.

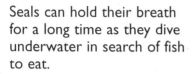

Seals

Sea
otter

Before going to sleep,
sea otters wind seaweed
round themselves so
that they won't drift
with the tide.

Sea lion

Sea lions are a kind of
seal. Since they can
turn their back flippers
to face forward, they
can move easily on land.

15

Small Sea Animals

Everything that lives in the sea must
find food. There are tiny creatures,
like krill and sea slugs, that eat sea
plants. Some big animals, like the
whale shark, also eat plants, but many
sea animals simply eat
other animals.

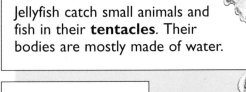

Jellyfish catch small animals and
fish in their **tentacles**. Their
bodies are mostly made of water.

Sea slugs can adapt
to very warm or
very cold water.

Starfish like to live in
shallow water and
in rock pools.

The largest animal in the sea is the blue whale, whose favourite food is krill. It gulps up huge mouthfuls of water. Then it lets the water drain out, keeping all the tiny krill in its mouth.

Krill are tiny shrimp-like animals that live in huge swarms. Although they can swim, they usually tend to drift.

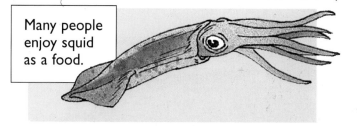

Many people enjoy squid as a food.

The ice fish has its own special protection against freezing because it lives in very cold water.

Sea Reptiles

Turtles, snakes and crocodiles all belong to a group of animals called **reptiles**. Reptiles lay eggs. Sea reptiles live in the warmer seas because they have no way of heating themselves up. In cold water they could only move very slowly. Reptiles are often called 'cold-blooded' animals.

Crocodiles have large jaws and sharp teeth. At sea, they often simply drift with the **currents**.

Sea crocodile

When turtles are frightened, they pull their heads and legs inside their tough, protective shells. Female turtles lay their eggs on the beach. When the baby turtles hatch about two months later, they rush down to the water and swim away.

This turtle's shell is made up of small bones, not bony plates like those of other turtles.

Leatherback turtle

Sea snake

Sea snakes are the most poisonous snakes in the world. They can swim very fast.

Sea Birds

Many sea birds live near the coast and catch fish from the sea. Nearly all have **webbed feet**.

Most sea birds make nests on land. The king penguin doesn't make a nest. Instead, the parents take turns holding the egg on their feet until it hatches. A special flap of skin comes down to keep the egg warm.

Puffins can hold a surprising number of fish in their colourful beaks. They like to eat herrings.

Puffins

Oystercatcher

This bird uses its beak like a hammer to break open shells.

Gannets dive deep into the water to catch fish. They dive with their wings folded.

Penguins cannot fly, but they are very good swimmers. They use their wings as flippers.

Penguin

Gannet

The cormorant has a hooked beak for gripping fish.

Cormorant

21

Whales

Whales are not fish. They are mammals, so they have to come to the surface to breathe. They blow out air through blowholes on the tops of their heads. Whales swim by moving their tails up and down in the water.

Minke whale

Minke whales are one of the smallest whales. They are only about as long as a car.

Beluga

Killer whale

The killer whale is the only whale that attacks and kills other whales.

Early sailors called the beluga whale the 'sea canary' because of the squeaky noises it makes.

Narwhal

Only the male narwhal has a long tusk, which is really a tooth that has grown out through its top lip.

Dolphins and Porpoises

Dolphins and porpoises are playful creatures. They enjoy playing and splashing in the water, or giving their **calves** piggyback rides. Sometimes they even race alongside boats.

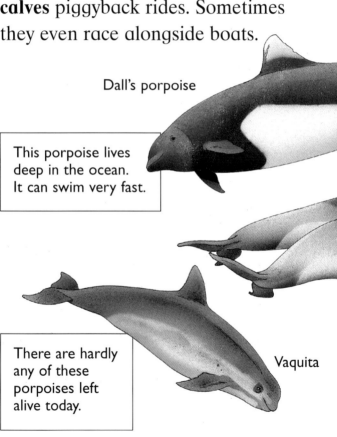

Dall's porpoise

This porpoise lives deep in the ocean. It can swim very fast.

There are hardly any of these porpoises left alive today.

Vaquita

The harbour porpoise
lives near the
coast in
northern
seas.

Harbour porpoise

This is the
biggest type of
dolphin. It has a
very large beak.

Bottlenose dolphin

Common dolphin

Dolphins use their teeth
to grip fish and squid. They
swallow their prey whole.

Coral Reef

Coral reefs have been formed from the skeletons of millions of tiny animals called corals. A third of all the fish in the world live around coral reefs.

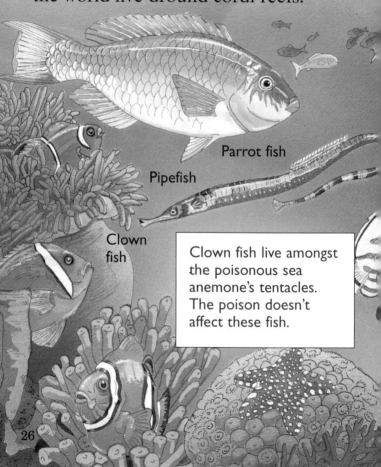

Parrot fish

Pipefish

Clown fish

Clown fish live amongst the poisonous sea anemone's tentacles. The poison doesn't affect these fish.

Triggerfish

The triggerfish can lock its sharp fin in an upright position to protect itself.

The moray eel hides in cracks in the coral reef. It darts out quickly to catch passing fish.

Moray eel

The sea horse is a strange looking fish. It can cling to seaweed with its tail to stop itself drifting.

Sea horse

Endangered Sea Animals

Whales, seals, turtles and dugongs are all **endangered** because they have been hunted for hundreds of years. Most countries now have laws to protect these animals from being hunted and killed.

Seal

Not long ago, seals were killed for their fur, to make clothes.

Sea bird

Oil spills affect all life in and on the sea: birds, animals and plants.

Year by year, there are fewer and fewer blue whales in the world, because so many are being killed.

Blue whale

For many years people had no respect for the sea. They dumped all their rubbish in it, causing **pollution**. Now some seas are very dirty, and animals and fish find it difficult to live there.

Some types of fish are becoming endangered because modern large fishing nets catch a great many more than ever before.

Waste from factories has been poured into the sea, killing fish and other animals

Toxic waste

Glossary

Adapt To change gradually over time.

Calf A term used for a young animal. Baby dolphins are called calves.

Current A movement of water under the surface in a sea or lake.

Endangered When an animal is endangered, it is in danger of dying out completely.

Evolve To develop or change over many years.

Flexible To bend easily.

Mammal An animal that breathes air and gives birth to live babies. Humans, walruses and whales are all mammals.

Mollusc An animal with a soft body that usually lives in a shell.

Pollution To make sea, land or air dirty and unfit for use.

Prey An animal hunted or killed by another animal for food.

Reptile A cold-blooded animal with a scaly skin. Most reptiles lay eggs.

Tentacle A long thin part of an animal's body, used for feeding, grasping or moving.

Tide The rise and fall of the sea that occurs twice a day.

Toxic Poisonous.

Webbed feet All the space between the toes is filled with skin, which helps the animal to swim.